A Christmas
in Slovakia

by Wesley Ellis

A Christmas in Slovakia
by Wesley Ellis

ISBN 0-9665175-9-8
LCCN: 2004109208

4661 Pinewood Drive, East
Mobile, Alabama 36618
Printed in the United States of America

Cover design and typesetting by Carolyn Miller Design

A Christmas in Slovakia

knew that it would be a Christmas different from any other I'd ever spent. The first reason was obvious: I had just begun teaching English in Czecho-Slovakia and I would be more than five thousand miles from home; away from family, friends, familiar surroundings.

Second, I would be in a country in which religion had been forcibly repressed for over forty years. True, the communist regime had fallen a scant year before but had its attempts at creating an atheistic state succeeded even to a small degree? Would the Slovaks celebrate the birth of our Lord? Would I be denied, for the first time in my adult life, the joy of attending one of the most important services of the Christian year: the Midnight Mass on Christmas Eve? I had already learned, from my teaching schedule, that we would have a holiday from December 22, 1990 through January 3, 1991 so they did celebrate something. But was it a sacred or a secular Christmas?

There were many questions about what to expect in Czecho-Slovakia. I already knew that during the holidays I would probably be the only person in the drab, deteriorating six-storey, concrete building in which my one-room apartment was located. It had been built by the communist regime to be used as a dormitory, housing the student apprentices at the leather factory next door. Mine, as near as I could determine, was the only non- student apartment in the building. Since the students would have returned to their homes for the holidays, I would be alone. Well, I thought, I'll just forget that it's Christmas. It'll just be another day. I'll go to Prague and try to lose myself in the holiday crowd.

Then I began seeing a few Christmas ornaments and decorations in the shop windows: a beautiful nativity scene, intricately crafted from straw; tiny angels made of silvery foil; brightly colored tree ornaments. Well, maybe it won't be so different after all, I thought, but will it be a purely commercial Christmas? Will the true spirit of the Lord's birth be evident?

It was now less than two weeks until Christmas. I bought a few ornaments to hang in my room as a feeble attempt to duplicate what I knew my family would be doing back home in the U.S. I tried to imagine my daughters, Leslie and Peggy, decorating their apartment in Birmingham where they and the rest of the family would gather for Christmas dinner, for the exchange of gifts, for laughter, closeness, and love. And together they would attend the Holy Eucharist at midnight on Christmas Eve.

I kept myself occupied by preparing lesson plans, writing letters, reading. I went sight-seeing. I hiked in the mountains around the small city which would be my home until Christmas was long past.

The author in Proslecka Valley near Liptovský Mikuláš, Slovak Republic

es, my family and I would like for you to spend Christmas Eve with us this year." I had met Jozef Čajka on my first morning in Liptovský Mikuláš, Czecho-Slovakia, now the Republic of Slovakia. "We want you to share with us a typical Slovak celebration of Christmas," Jozef continued. What a welcomed invitation! Immediately, the gray skies seemed brighter and Liptovský Mikuláš didn't appear so drab anymore. My room even began to look a little more festive. I would not be alone on Christmas! I walked with a lighter step. But the question remained: would I be able to worship the birth of Jesus on Christmas Eve? I wondered if Jozef had succumbed to the persistent and persuasive atheistic indoctrination by the communist regime. Was he one of those who fell for the there-is-no-God propaganda? His invitation to a *traditional* Slovak Christmas indicated that he felt in his heart the spirit of giving and sharing. And if it was traditional, then it probably predated the communist takeover of his country. I knew, too, from the ubiquitous onion-domed churches there, that the Slovak people had a strong Christian heritage.

The week before Christmas, I went to Bratislava with Róbert Kasanicky, a young Slovak who was my interpreter, my tour guide and friend. In retrospect, I'm sure that Róbert helped to fill the emptiness I felt at being separated from my family at Christmas. (Róbert and my son, John, are about the same age.) Perhaps I filled a need in Róbert's life, too, because his father had died the previous year.

As we stood on the balcony of the Hotel Carlton, where I was staying in Bratislava, a choral group in Hviezdoslav Square below began singing Christmas carols. The clear, well-trained voices filled the square with beautiful music. I heard a melody that I recognized: the lilting *Nesiem vám noviny (Come, all ye shepherds)*, a Moravian carol, very popular in Czecho-Slovakia and fairly well-known in the U.S. The choir performed a program of beautiful selections which I assumed were popular carols in Slovakia. But there were none of the old, familiar Christmas favorites we would hear back home. Róbert, too, was lost in the music. After the choir finished singing, he turned to me and, with tears in his eyes, said "This is the first Christmas that we've been permitted to hear Christmas music in public."

From that moment on, I knew that this Christmas would be one of the most memorable and meaningful of my life.

Triptych in the Gothic Church in Smrečany, near Liptovský Mikuláš, Slovak Republic

Left to right: Hanka Takáčová (Jana's daughter), Hanka's cousin, the author, Jana Takáčová

oon after we returned from our trip to Bratislava, the holiday season was further brightened with an invitation to have lunch on Christmas Day with [1]Jana Takáčová and her family: her daughter, parents, siblings and their families. It was a family celebration, but as an "adopted" member, I was included, too. Being with this close, loving family would help significantly to ease the void left by my being apart from my own loved ones at this special time of the year.

I was beginning to appreciate more fully the true nature of Slovak hospitality!

1 A few of Jana's special Christmas recipes are found at the end of this book, beginning on page17.

Jozef Čajka, his mother and little daughter, Monika

ozef picked me up late afternoon on Christmas Eve and we headed for his family's *chata* (cabin), near the small village of Bobrovec at the base of the High Tatra Mountains. Awaiting us at the cabin were Jozef's wife, his mother and his two small children. The two women had spent the day—and probably many previous days—preparing the sumptuous feast that was to follow.

The evening began with toasts to U.S.-Slovak friendship, to our families, to Christmas, and to anything else we could think of to salute. The drink was a traditional apéritif, [2]*hriatô*, served warm and over bacon bits. It was quite a new taste experience for me. After this toast, there was the traditional clove of garlic for good health during the coming year, and a few coins under the corner of the tablecloth for wealth.

Then, with a meal which lasted for over four and a half hours, the Slovak Christmas celebration began in earnest. The first course was a small plate of appetizers, somewhat like sweetened dumplings covered with

2 See page 23 for recipe.

poppy seed. After this followed a soup which I was to learn later was a traditional Christmas soup in that area of Slovakia. As near as I could determine, it was made of homemade sauerkraut (nothing like the canned variety we have in the U.S.), sausage, potatoes, noodles, onions and is very tasty.[3]

As we were finishing the soup course, Jozef's lighthearted behavior of the evening changed as he became more serious. Hesitantly, as if he wasn't sure how to put his question into words, he said, "Wes, after our Christmas dinner, we are going to midnight mass and we wondered if you would like to go with us, or do you want me to take you back to your apartment?"

How could I express the joy his invitation had created within me? Did I want to go to church on Christmas Eve? "Of course," I told him, "I want to go with you." It was an inadequate response to convey the surge of happiness I felt.

The lighthearted atmosphere that had typified the evening returned to the *chata* as the festivities continued. Jozef's wife and mother brought in the next course: grilled, fresh trout with boiled potatoes, potato

3 See page 25 for recipe.

salad, and pickled mushrooms. This was topped off with a fruit compote of cherries, apricots, mandarin orange slices.

While the children were opening their gifts and the adults relaxed, Jozef asked me if I would like the sweets now or after the main course. I nearly collapsed for I thought we had just finished the main course. I had consumed enough for two people. I could hardly move. Weakly, though, I managed a smile and told him that whatever was traditional would be fine with me. His mother appeared with two large trays of sweets: filled pastries, pinwheels, elaborately decorated cookies and small cakes—treats which were almost too beautiful to eat. We feasted on these and I tried my best to save a little room for the finale. After another brief respite, out came the sixth and, I prayed, the final course. It consisted of breaded cutlets and a reappearance of the earlier accompanying dishes of potatoes and mushrooms, plus a salad of fresh lettuce—a rarity in Slovakia at that time of year—and cooked, pickled soya beans. Jozef commented that the latter dish was the only non-traditional food of the evening.

Interspersed into this more than five-hour session of

The Čajka family gathers for the Christmas dinner

culinary extravaganza were the giving and receiving of gifts, picture taking, more toasts with wine or apéritifs, conversation, coffee and tea. About midway through the evening, the extended family began coming in to share their Christmas greetings. There were sisters, brothers, in-laws, aunts, uncles, cousins, nieces and nephews. The room was filled with laughter, joy and love. And not once was I ever made to feel like an outsider. Jozef and I were the only ones who spoke English, but the entire family more than communicated the Christmas spirit in a language that needed no translation.

The dinner ended with a champagne toast after which we set off for the small, tenth-century church in the village of Bobrovec. It was already packed when we arrived and we had to stand in the narthex for the entire service. But that was unimportant. What did it matter that there were no available seats? For me, the important thing was that I was in church on Christmas Eve. I was celebrating the Lord's birth. How can I describe the overwhelming, but humbling, feeling of being with these gentle, compassionate people and knowing that this was the first Christmas in more than forty years when they could openly worship their Lord without fear of persecution or reprisal?

The service was in Slovak, of course, but some parts of the mass are easily recognizable in any language: the Gloria, the Creed, the passing of the Peace, the Sanctus. Then suddenly, near the end of the mass, I knew that my Christmas was complete. The words were in the language of my fellow worshippers, but I was surrounded by the soft strains of the music which unites Christians around the world at Christmas time:

> *Tichá noc, svätá noc!*
> *Všetko spí, všetko sní,*
> *sám len svätý bdie dôverný pár,*
> *stráži Dieťatko, nebeský dar.*
> *Sladký Ježiško spí, sní,*
> *nebeský ticho spí, sní.*
>
> *Silent night, holy night!*
> *All is calm, all is bright,*
> *Round yon Virgin Mother and Child.*
> *Holy Infant, so tender and mild.*
> *Sleep in heavenly peace,*
> *Sleep in heavenly peace.*

Christmas Recipes from Slovakia

by

Jana Takáčová

ABOUT CHRISTMAS SAUERKRAUT SOUP
by Jana Takáčová

Every cook has her or his own way of preparing this traditional soup. Instead of sauerkraut, some families use lentil soup as a base; some use the sauerkraut only while others use only the strained juice.

I often wondered why it is such a special soup. Until recently, we used to cook this soup a month in advance, as a sort of a rehearsal. It gave the day a festive atmosphere. In our family and in our village, it has always been considered to be a festive rather than an every-day meal.

Traditionally, our Christmas sauerkraut soup is served with home-made noodles and a piece of potato. In some villages, the preferred pasta is quite special, and not everyone is able to make it, unless given hands-on-training.

It has always been served at Christmas Eve, and if we were lucky, there would be some left for Christmas day. We come from a mostly Lutheran region where meat is eaten at the evening meal on Christmas Eve, unlike the

Catholics who would abstain from meat or a meat soup until Christmas Day.

The sour taste of the soup may be a novelty for American palates. In introducing a recipe to a family, it is my experience that it helps to let them get really hungry before serving a new dish for the first time.

Being so special, this soup is also served at New Year's Eve in our family.

My estimate for best proportion of ingredients used may vary according to one's own taste.

Christmas Sauerkraut Soup

1 pkg. noodles (broad egg, dumpling, etc.)
1½ qts. strained sauerkraut
3 qts. water
1-2 lbs fresh, lean pork
1 lb. smoked pork (optional)
5 dried plums [prunes] (optional)
2 large onions, quartered
4 garlic cloves, halved
4 bay leaves

2 T. dried mushrooms *(in the U.S. probably*
known under the German name, Steinpilz)
½ t. caraway seeds
1 t. sweet red paprika
Salt to taste
2-4 links smoked sausage
4-6 large potatoes, halved

Cook the noodles in water according to directions on package, then drain, rinse and set aside.

Place remaining ingredients, except the sausages and potatoes, in a large pot and bring to a boil. Lower heat and simmer for approximately 1 hour. Add the sausages. Simmer for another 30 minutes. Add the potatoes and simmer for 30 minutes more, chasing away those coming and asking what this wonderful meal is going to be.

When ready to serve, place the cooked noodles in a soup tureen, pour the hot soup over and serve immediately.

There is not much more you need for the second course. The usual serving is a piece of boiled meat, a piece of sausage, boiled in the soup while it is cooking; a couple of potatoes, a vegetable. Our favorite addition is a portion of *Wienerschnitzel* and mashed potatoes.

A good walk is recommended afterwards.

An upgraded version of this delicacy is what we call *Kura slepá*. It is, in fact, a dumpling prepared from ingredients you would use for a chicken stuffing, and added to this soup in the last phase of simmering.

Kura Slepá
(Sauerkraut Soup Dumplings)

4 hard rolls, cut in cubes
  (2- or 3-day old bread may be substituted)
1 thick slice bacon, cut in small cubes
1 onion, chopped
2 c. flour
4 eggs
Parsley, finely chopped
3 cloves garlic, finely chopped
Salt to taste

Sprinkle water over the cubed rolls or bread and let stand. Sauté lightly one half of the bacon cubes with one half the chopped onion. Let cool.

In a large bowl, mix together all the ingredients, including the cooked as well as the uncooked bacon cubes and chopped onion. Stir lightly with a wooden spoon. With wet palms, form into either small balls or two loaves. Place in the sauerkraut soup to cook, turning over when halfway done (cooking time approximately 10 minutes for the balls, 15-20 minutes for the loaves). Check for doneness by cutting a piece crosswise. Do not overcook. Remove from soup, cover to keep warm and serve with the main course.

ABOUT HRIATÔ

This aperitif is a speciality of the mountainous region of Liptov in northern Slovakia where the altitude ranges from 500 to 2050 meters [1640 to 6725 feet] above sea level and the climate is rather cold. This should be borne in mind as the drink was probably meant to warm people up at Christmas time when they came in from outside, working in the barn or feeding cattle, for example. This drink is a savory reminder of our grandparents' homes and their duties and pleasures.

Hriatô means a warm drink. It used to be prepared at special occasions only, such as Christmas time. Never more than one or two liqueur-glass servings were drunk. It is not a drink to be diluted by ice, soft drink, or soda. And never served in a tall glass.

It is unusual in several ways: it contains fat, it is drunk hot, and it tastes both sweet and salty. Again, this may not necessarily go with the [lack of] physical exertion of present-day society. It is, indeed, a wintertime apéritif, well-established in cold climates.

In preparing it, care should be taken in observing the proper sequence to avoid fire.

Hriatô
(Serves two)

2 T. small bacon cubes
2 T. sugar
2 dl (about 4 jiggers or 3 oz.) vodka
1 dl (about 2 jiggers or 1″ oz.) water

Fry the bacon cubes, drain and set aside. In a heavy skillet, caramelize the sugar to a *very light* brown color only. Remove from heat and allow to cool for a minute. Add water. Return to heat and simmer until the caramel dissolves. Slowly add vodka. Divide the bacon cubes and place in the bottom of two apéritif glasses. Pour the hot drink over. Serve immediately.

For vegetarians, *hriatô* may be served without the bacon.

Sauerkraut - Slovak Style

(If you'd like to try your hand at making sauerkraut the way the Slovaks do, Jana Takáčová has graciously shared her family recipe.)

Preparing your crock and tools:

For best results, you'll need a large (at least 8- to 10-gallon) earthenware crock in which to make it. Do not use aluminum as the acidity of the cabbage mixture will cause a metallic contamination. A cover is necessary, and if the crock does not come with one, a heavy plate or wood disk, slightly smaller than the opening will work.

It is very important that the crock, the utensils or tools used—anything that will come in contact with the cabbage mixture—be absolutely clean. Wash them thoroughly with **very hot** water ONLY—no soap, detergent or other cleaning material lest they contaminate the mixture and interfere with the fermentation process. After scrubbing with hot water, rinse well with cold water.

Ingredients *(all amounts are approximate):*
>
> 65 lbs. cabbage
>
> 6 lbs. onions, peeled
>
> 1 lb. salt
>
> Several bay leaves
>
> 2 or 3 T. caraway seeds
>
> Black pepper
>
> Red beets, sliced (optional)
>
> Fresh horseradish, chopped
>
> Several hard apples, such as Granny Smith or Winesap, for flavor

Note: You may make a smaller amount, but keep the proportions approximately the same. Jana tells the story of one of her friends who married an Englishman and she became so homesick in Britain for Slovak sauerkraut that she made a batch with a single head of cabbage, using a four-liter jug!

Preparing the Kraut:

Remove the dry or dirty outer leaves of the heads of cabbage, then cut into quarters, remove and discard the core. Shred or cut into thin slices. There is a special machine for this purpose in Slovakia, but a food processor will work, too.

In a large vat or tub, mix together with your hands all the ingredients except the horseradish and apples. The beets are optional and are added if you want red colored sauerkraut.

Spread the chopped horseradish on the bottom of the crock, then begin layering the mixture, adding an apple (for flavor) between layers. Each layer must be pressed or punched down hard with a tight fist or, if you have one, a wooden tool made especially for this purpose. Do not fill the crock too full, but give the kraut room for fermentation and expansion.

Fermentation Phase I:

For the initial stage, place the crock, covered with a clean cloth, in a warm spot to speed up the process. But be forewarned that the fermenting kraut gives off a rather pungent odor, so you may want to find a secluded or isolated spot for it to do its work!

Fermentation Phase II:

Check the sauerkraut regularly (every day or two), especially in the earlier stages. You will probably see a small, white growth; this is normal, but it should be carefully removed. There will also be abundant foaming caused by the fermenting process at first; when this ceases, after a few days, the sauerkraut should be tightly covered with a lid and moved to a cooler spot.

The fermentation phase produces much liquid and it may be necessary from time to time to ladle some of it off the top, but *do not* throw it out. Store it in the refrigerator, using it to replace any liquid lost later in the fermenting process. Also the juice is valued by the Slovaks as a digestive aid. The cabbage should not be allowed to become dry on the top—make sure there is a thin layer of liquid covering it at all times, using some of the reserved liquid if necessary.

A plate or wooden circle should be used to weigh down the sauerkraut, using a heavy weight (a *clean,* round stone works well) on top of the plate to maintain the heavy, downward pressure, keeping the kraut below the surface of the liquid.

The preparation of homemade sauerkraut, Slovak style, is somewhat time-consuming, but well worth the effort.

There is a saying in Slovakia,

"When the cellar is stocked with sauerkraut, potatoes, smoked sausage, apples and coal, then winter can begin!"

*Portrait of the author painted in 1993 by Herb Ethan, an
internationally known artist now living in San Miguel de Allende.*

Wesley Ellis was born in Selma and grew up in Auburn,
Alabama. After serving in the US Army, he received his
bachelors degree from Auburn University and then obtained
his masters from Louisiana State University. For many years,
he was organist and choirmaster at a number of churches in
Auburn, Mobile, Baton Rouge and Seneca, SC.

Ellis did additional study in languages and writing at
the University of South Alabama. In addition to Slovakia, he
has lived in San Miguel de Allende, Mexico. Father of three
children and five grandchildren, he currently lives in
Auburn.